To Jimmy Zazzali, a great golfer who will not admit it,
F.X. (Buddy) Keegan, Peter Nelson,
Nelson Iannarone, Jim Mackey (who has a green jacket),
Howard "Mr. Hole-in-One" Wilson,
W. G. Anderson (great guy, great golfer),
Alex Giordano and, of course,
my favorite golfer and caddy—Hymie "Tiger" Lipschitz.

Acknowledgments

A special thanks to Sara Kase and Peter Lynch at Sourcebooks, Erin Mackey for her loyal assistance, William "Doc" Sullivan, Robert Sufferdini, Phil Milot, Ed Carchia, Bobby Beck, Sylvester Larena, John McMahon, Tom Crowley, Governor Richard J. Codey, and especially Jaclyn Marie Foley for letting me out of the house, and Ryan Foley for not carrying golf clubs.

GOD LOVES GOLFERS BEST

The Best Jokes,
Quotes, and Cartoons
for Golfers

RAY FOLEY

SOURCEBOOKS, INC.®
NAPERVILLE, ILLINOIS

Published by Sourcebooks, Inc.
P.O. Box 4410, Naperville, Illinois 60567-4410
(630) 961-3900
Fax: (630) 961-2168
www.sourcebooks.com

Library of Congress Cataloging-in-Publication Data
Foley, Ray.
  God loves golfers best : the best jokes, quotes, and cartoons for golfers / Ray Foley.
      p. cm.
  1. Golf--Humor. 2. Golf--Quotations, maxims, etc. 3. Golf--Caricatures and cartoons. I. Title. II. Title: Best jokes, quotes, and cartoons for golfers.
  PN6231.G68F65 2009
  818'.602--dc22
                          2008047798

Printed and bound in the United States of America
VP 10 9 8 7 6 5 4

Golf Course or...

Four married guys go golfing. While playing the 4th hole, the following conversation takes place:

1st Guy: "You have no idea what I had to do to be able to come out golfing this weekend. I had to promise my wife that I would paint every room in the house next weekend."

2nd Guy: "That's nothing. I had to promise my wife I would build a new deck for the pool."

3rd Guy: "Man, you both have it easy! I had to promise my wife I would remodel the kitchen for her."

They continued to play the hole when they realized that the 4th guy hadn't said anything. So they asked him, "You haven't said anything about what you had to do to be able to come golfing this weekend. What's the deal?"

4th Guy: "I just set my alarm for 5:30 a.m. and when it went off, I shut off the alarm, gave the wife a nudge, and said, 'Golf course or intercourse?'

And she said, 'Wear your sweater.'"

"CONCEDE THE STROKE ALREADY, HARRY!"

> **"'Play it as it lies' is one of the fundamental dictates of golf. The other is, 'Wear it if it clashes.'"**
>
> —Henry Beard

 Late Arrival

One golfer asked his friend, "Why are you arriving so late for your tee time?"

His friend replied, "It's Sunday. I had to toss a coin between going to church and playing golf."

"Yes," continued the friend, "but that still doesn't tell me why you are so late."

"Well," said the fellow, "it took over twenty-five tosses to get it right!"

What to Do

Earl addressed the ball and took a magnificent swing, but somehow, something went wrong and a horrible slice resulted. The ball went onto the adjoining fairway and hit a man full force. He dropped! Earl and his partner ran up to the stricken victim, who lay unconscious with the ball between his feet.

"Good heavens," exclaimed Earl, "what shall I do?"

"Don't move him," said his partner. "If we leave him here, he becomes an immovable obstruction, and you can either play the ball as it lies or take a two-club-length drop."

> ## "I'd give up golf if I didn't have so many sweaters."
>
> —Bob Hope

👉 Marriage

A man is getting married and is standing by his bride at the church. Standing beside him are his golf clubs and bag.

His bride whispers, "What are your golf clubs doing here?"

The groom replies, "This isn't going to take all day, is it?"

Tough Round

A man comes home after a terrible round of golf, his worst ever. He plops down on the couch in front of the television and tells his wife, "Get me a beer before it starts."

The wife sighs and gets him a beer.

Fifteen minutes later, he says, "Get me another beer before it starts." She looks cross but fetches another beer and slams it down next to him. He finishes that beer and a few minutes later says, "Quick, get me another beer, it's going to start any minute."

The wife is furious. She yells at him, "You've been out golfing all day! Is that all you're going to do tonight? Drink beer and sit in front of that TV? You're nothing but a lazy, drunken, fat slob, and furthermore…"

The man sighs and says, "It's started…"

"FOUR! ... FIVE! ... SIX! ... SEVEN!"

"Everybody has two swings—a beautiful practice swing and the choked-up one with which they hit the ball. So it wouldn't do either of us a damned bit of good to look at your practice swing."

—Ed Furgol

"The difference between golf and government is that in golf you can't improve your lie."

—George Deukmejian

"We speak of eyeball-to-eyeball encounters between men great and small. Even more reaching and revealing of character is the eyeball-to-golf-ball confrontation, whereby our most secret natures are mercilessly tested by a small, round, whitish object with no mind or will but with a very definite life of its own, and with whims perverse and beatific."

—John Stewart Martin

☞ Bullish on Trousers

Why did the golfer take an extra pair of pants when he went out on the golf course?

Just in case he got a hole in one.

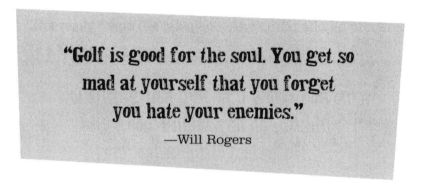

"Golf is good for the soul. You get so mad at yourself that you forget you hate your enemies."

—Will Rogers

👉 Golfer and Caddie

Golfer: "How do you like my game?"

Caddie: "Very good, sir, but personally, I prefer golf."

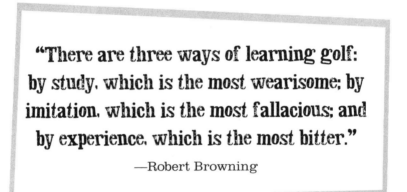

"There are three ways of learning golf: by study, which is the most wearisome; by imitation, which is the most fallacious; and by experience, which is the most bitter."

—Robert Browning

"BAD ENOUGH SHE GOT THE HOUSE, THE CAR, AND THE KIDS, THE JUDGE ALSO GAVE HER CUSTODY OF MY STARTING TIME!"

"If you call on God to improve the results of a shot while it is still in motion, you are using 'an outside agency' and are subject to appropriate penalties under the rules of golf."

—Henry Longhurst

Funeral Procession

Mike, an avid golfer, was teeing up for a very difficult shot. At that moment, a funeral procession went by. Mike stopped, stood still with his hat over his heart, and bowed his head. His golfing partner looked at him and said, "Mike, that was kind and decent of you to show such respect for the dead."

Mike replied, "Yes, we would have been married twenty-six years come tomorrow."

"Victory is everything. You can spend the money, but you can never spend the memories."

—Ken Venturi

> **"I'd like to see the fairways more narrow. Then everybody would have to play from the rough, not just me."**
>
> —Seve Ballesteros

 ## That's Not My Ball

"That can't be my ball, caddie. It looks far too old," said the player looking at a ball deep in the trees.

"It's a long time since we started, sir."

He's Not My Caddie

Rich Texans are fabled for their grand style, but when one oil tycoon appeared at a local British golf course followed by a servant pulling a foam-cushioned chaise lounge, his opponents thought that this was taking style too far.

"J.R., are you going to make that poor caddie lug that couch all over the course after you?" they asked him.

"Caddie, my eye," explained J.R. "That's my psychiatrist."

"The harder you work, the luckier you get."

—Gary Player

"You've just one problem. You stand too close to the ball after you've hit it."

—Sam Snead

"PAR IS 68! THIS ISN'T SO TOUGH, I'VE BEEN UNDER PAR ON ALMOST EVERY HOLE!"

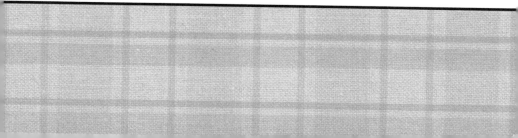

From a Huge Slice...

Talk about fantastic golf teachers. He was the best, and one day this woman came to him and said that she had developed a terrific slice. Day and night he worked with her for five months.

Now she's the biggest hooker in town.

> "The only time my prayers are never answered is on the golf course."
>
> —Billy Graham

☞ Stop Checking the Time

"Please stop checking your watch all the time, caddie. It's distracting!"

"This isn't a watch, sir. It's a compass!"

I'll Sue You

A golfer is ready to tee off, when a golfer in the adjacent fairway hits him square in the face with his golf ball.

"Idiot! Your ball hit me in the eye! I'll sue you for five million dollars!"

The other golfer replied, "I said 'fore!'"

The first golfer then said, "I'll take it!"

☞ Who Do You Think You Are?

Jesus and Arnold Palmer are playing golf. Arnold tees off. It's a long drive straight up the fairway, and he's about a 5-iron off the green.

"Not bad," Jesus says. Jesus steps up to tee off, but his drive slices badly and lands on an island in the middle of a water hazard. Jesus calmly walks across the water to take his next shot.

"Jesus!" yells Palmer, "who do you think you are, Jack Nicklaus?"

> **"Golf is a game in which you yell 'fore,' shoot six, and write down five."**
>
> —Paul Harvey

"TOUGHEST COURSE I'VE EVER PLAYED!"

My Wife Left Me

Fred called his friend in tears. "I can't believe it," he sobbed. "My wife left me for my golfing partner."

"Get a hold of yourself, man," said his friend. "There are plenty of other women out there."

"Who's talking about her?" said Fred. "He was the only guy that I could ever beat!"

> **"A professional will tell you the amount of flex you need in the shaft of your club. The more the flex, the more strength you will need to break the thing over your knees."**
>
> —Stephen Baker

> **"Every rock 'n' roll band I know, guys with long hair and tattoos, plays golf now."**
>
> —Alice Cooper

"**Golf** is **20** percent mechanics and technique. The other **80** percent is philosophy, humor, tragedy, romance, melodrama, companionship, camaraderie, cussedness, and conversation."

—Grantland Rice

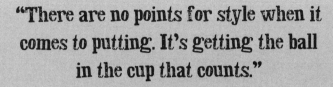

> **"There are no points for style when it comes to putting. It's getting the ball in the cup that counts."**
>
> —Brian Swarbrick

👉 She'll Leave Me

"My wife says she's leaving me if I don't give up golf."

"What are you going to do?"

"Miss her like hell."

Neither Would He

My wife asked me why I don't play golf with Patrick anymore. So I asked her, "Would you continue to play with a guy who always gets drunk, loses so many balls other groups are always playing through, tells lousy jokes while you are trying to putt, and generally offends everyone around him on the course?"

"Certainly not, dear," she replied.

"Well, neither would he."

> ## "Putts get real difficult the day they hand out the money."
> —Lee Trevino

"HONEY, TELL ME ABOUT THE TIME YOU HIT THAT HOLE
IN ONE. I'M HAVING TROUBLE FALLING ASLEEP!"

"Obviously a deer on the fairway has seen you tee off before and knows that the safest place to be when you play is right down the middle."

—Jackie Gleason

Drag George

A fellow comes home after golf one Sunday afternoon, falls asleep on the couch, and doesn't wake up until about 9:00 p.m. His wife asks why he is so tired.

"Well, you remember George, my golfing buddy? He died today on the 4th green."

"That's terrible, it must have been awful," she says.

"It sure was," he says. "For the next 14 holes it was drive, drag George, chip, drag George, putt, drag George..."

**"I've spent most of my life golfing.
The rest I've just wasted."**

—Unknown

👉 I'm Drowning

Misjudging its depth, Ron waded into the lake to retrieve his badly sliced ball. Very quickly he was floundering out of his depth and, as his tweed plus-fours became waterlogged, he found himself in real trouble.

"Help, I'm drowning!" he shouted to his partner.

"Don't worry," came the reply. "You won't drown. You'll never keep your head down long enough."

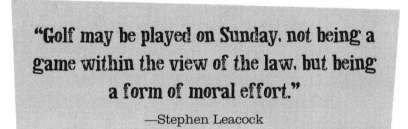

"Golf may be played on Sunday, not being a game within the view of the law, but being a form of moral effort."

—Stephen Leacock

Emergency

"Doctor, we've got an emergency! My baby just swallowed my golf tees."

"I'll be there at once."

"But tell me what to do 'til you get here, doc?"

"Practice your putting."

"IT'S AN OPEN AND SHUT CASE OF DRIVING
UNDER THE INFLUENCE!"

☞ Only Golfers Allowed

Eric, the club's worst golfer, was addressing his ball. Feet apart, just so, eye on the ball, just so, a few practice wiffles with the driver, just so, and then swing. He missed. Eric repeated the procedure and then repeated it again. On the fourth swing, however, he did manage to connect with his ball and drove it five meters down the fairway. Looking up in exasperation, he saw a stranger who had stopped to watch him.

"Look here!" Eric shouted angrily. "Only golfers are allowed on this course!"

The stranger nodded, "I know it, mister," he replied, "but I won't say anything if you won't either!"

**"Most golfers prepare for disaster.
A good golfer prepares for success."**

—Bob Toski

A Scratch Golfer

Two women were put together as partners in the club tournament and met on the putting green for the first time.

After introductions, the first golfer asked, "What's your handicap?"

"Oh, I'm a scratch golfer," the other replied.

"Really!" exclaimed the first woman, suitably impressed that she was paired up with her.

"Yes, I write down all my good scores and scratch out the bad ones!"

"Golf is a game where guts and blind devotion will always net you absolutely nothing but an ulcer."

—Tommy Bolt

A Golfer's Wife

The golfer's wife was in full flight. "If you ever spent a Sunday with me instead of playing golf I swear I would drop dead," she screamed.

"There's no point in trying to bribe me," replied her husband.

Lost and Found

"I say, greenskeeper, I dropped my bottle of Scotch out of the bag somewhere on the 7th. Anything handed in at lost-and-found?"

"Only the golfer who played after you, sir."

> ## "The average golfer doesn't play golf. He attacks it."
>
> —Jack Burke

"FORE!"

☞ What's My Handicap?

He was a smooth operator, and at the club's annual dance, he attached himself to the prettiest lady golfer in the room and was boasting to her.

"You know, they're all afraid to play me. What do you think my handicap is?"

"Well, where do you want me to start?" came the quick response.

> **"A golf course outside a big town serves an
> excellent purpose in that it segregates,
> as though in a concentration camp,
> all the idle and idiot well-to-do."**
>
> —Sir Osbert Sitwell

 Wife & Mistress

"I'll go and ask if we can play through," said Max to Jerry. The two golfers had been concerned for some time about the snail-like progress of two women who had originally been some holes ahead and were now just in front of them on the 9th fairway.

Max returned after only a few paces toward the ladies.

"Jerry, this is very embarrassing, but would you mind going? That's my wife up ahead, and she's playing with my mistress."

Jerry set out, only to return seconds later, having gotten no farther forward than Max.

"I say," he said, "what a coincidence."

"A day spent in a round of strenuous idleness."

—William Wordsworth

"I wasn't this nervous playing golf when I was drinking. It's the first tournament I've won on the **PGA** Tour in a sober manner, so it's a great feeling knowing I can do it sober. I don't think two years ago I could have pulled this off."

—John Daly

LOFT

Three aspiring golfers were taking lessons from a pro. The first guy hit the ball far to the right. "That was due to LOFT," said the pro.

The second man hit his ball far to the left. "That, too, was due to LOFT," said the pro.

The third golfer took a swing, and the ball just went a few feet and stopped. "Once again, it's LOFT," the pro claimed.

"Well, what exactly do you mean by LOFT?" asked the third golfer.

"Lack of fine talent," replied the pro.

"Golf is an awkward set of bodily contortions designed to produce a graceful result."
—Tommy Armour

Low Eighties

"I play golf in the low eighties," the old man was telling one of the youngsters at his club.

"Wow," said the young man, "that's pretty impressive."

"Not really," said the old man. "Any hotter and I'd probably have a stroke."

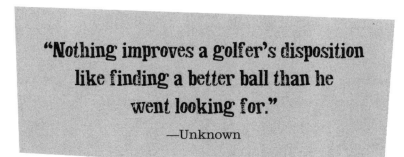

"Nothing improves a golfer's disposition like finding a better ball than he went looking for."

—Unknown

"IT'S JUST LIKE ELLIOT TO SPOIL
A GOOD SUNDAY MORNING!"

Could Have Been Worse

"Hey, George, did you hear the awful news about John?" The two golfers were talking over a drink in the club bar.

"No what happened to him?"

"Well, he had a great round on Wednesday—under seventy, I heard—anyway, he finished early and drove home and found his wife in bed with another man! No questions asked...he just shot 'em both! Isn't it terrible?"

"Could have been worse," George commented.

"How?"

"If he'd finished early on Tuesday, he would have shot me!"

> **"As an intellectual he bestowed upon the games of golf and bridge all the enthusiasm and perseverance that he withheld from books and ideas."**
>
> —Emmet John Hughes, on Dwight D. Eisenhower

"Eighteen holes of match play will teach you more about your foe than nineteen years of dealing with him across the desk."

—Grantland Rice

The Perfect Shot

A guy stood over his tee shot for what seemed an eternity; looking up, looking down, measuring the distance, figuring the wind direction and speed, and driving his partner nuts.

Finally his exasperated partner said, "What's taking so long? Hit the blasted ball."

The guy answered, "My wife is up there watching me from the clubhouse. I want to make this a perfect shot."

"Forget it; you don't stand a chance of hitting her from here."

"It's nice to have the opportunity to play for so much money, but it's nicer to win it."

—Patty Sheehan

"Always keep in mind that if God didn't want a man to have mulligans, golf balls wouldn't come three to a sleeve."

—Dan Jenkins

☞ The Golfer and His Bride

Two old folks get married. As they are laying in their wedding suite, staring at the ceiling, the old man says, "I haven't been completely honest with you. I think the world of you, but you are only number two to me. Golf is my first love. It's my hobby, my passion, my first love."

They both stare at the ceiling for a bit longer and then the woman says, "While we're baring our souls, I guess I better tell you that I have been a hooker all my life."

The man jumps out of bed, looks at her a moment, and then says, "Have you tried widening your stance and adjusting your grip?"

"WELL, IT LOOKS LIKE THIS BAD WEATHER WILL PUT A CRIMP IN YOUR GOLF MATCH."

☞ Blind Golf

A priest, a doctor, and a professional golfer were waiting one morning for a particularly slow group of golfers.

Golfer: "What's with these guys? We must have been waiting for fifteen minutes!"

Doctor: "I don't know but I've never seen such ineptitude!"

Priest: "Hey, here comes the greenskeeper. Let's have a word with him. Hi, George. Say, George, what's with that group ahead of us? They're rather slow, aren't they?"

George: "Oh yes. That's a group of blind firefighters. They lost their sight while saving our clubhouse last year, so we let them play here anytime, free of charge!"

(Silence)

Priest: "That's so sad. I think I will say a special prayer for them tonight."

Doctor: "Good idea. And I'm going to contact my ophthalmologist buddy and see if there's anything he can do for them."

Golfer: "Why can't these guys play at night?"

Hoover

Father Murphy was playing golf with a parishioner. On the 1st hole, he sliced into the rough. His opponent heard him mutter, "Hoover!" under his breath.

On the 2nd hole, Father Murphy's ball went straight into a water hazard. "Hoover!" again, a little louder this time.

On the 3rd hole, a miracle occurred, and Father Murphy's drive landed on the green only six inches from the hole! "Praise be to God!"

He carefully lined up the putt, but the ball curved around the hole instead of going in. "*Hoover!*"

By this time, his opponent couldn't withhold his curiosity any longer, and asked why the priest said, "Hoover."

"It's the biggest dam I know."

"Golf is based on honesty; where else would you admit to a seven on a par three?"

—Jimmy Demaret

Pregnant Golf

The room was full of pregnant women and their partners, and the Lamaze class was in full swing. The instructor was teaching the women how to breathe properly, along with informing the men how to give the necessary assurances at this stage of the plan.

The teacher then announced, "Ladies, exercise is good for you. Walking is especially beneficial. And gentlemen, it wouldn't hurt you to take the time to go walking with your partner!"

The room got quiet. Finally, a man in the middle of the group raised his hand.

"Yes?" replied the teacher.

"Is it all right if she carries a golf bag while we walk?"

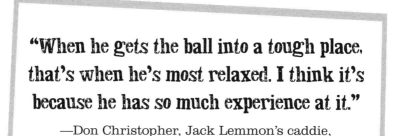

Clubs

After a not-so-terrific game, Dan and I were heading toward the clubhouse for drinks. I said to Dan, "What do you think I should give my caddie?"

Dan replied under his breath, "How about your clubs?"

> "When he gets the ball into a tough place, that's when he's most relaxed. I think it's because he has so much experience at it."
>
> —Don Christopher, Jack Lemmon's caddie,
> on Jack Lemmon

☞ Sunday

In the United States, Sunday is the day that most of us bow our heads. Some are in church—the rest are out playing golf.

"Why am I using a new putter? Because the last one didn't float too well."

—Craig Stadler

"All it takes to upset a serious golfer is one high ball."

—Unknown

Stop Nagging

"Mildred, shut up," cried the golfer at his nagging wife, "Shut up or you'll drive me out of my mind!"

"That," said Mildred, "wouldn't be a drive; it would be a short putt."

👉 True to Form

The police arrived and found a woman dead on her living room floor with a golf club next to her body. They asked the husband, "Is this your wife?"

"Yes," he replied.

"Did you kill her?"

"Yes," he replied.

"It looks like you struck her eight times with this 3-iron. Is that correct?"

"Well, yes," he replied, "...but could you put me down for five?"

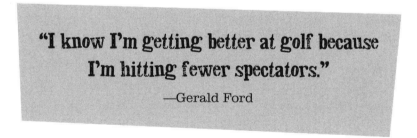

"I know I'm getting better at golf because I'm hitting fewer spectators."

—Gerald Ford

Weekend

I was talking with two of my coworkers last Monday morning at work.

"What did you do this weekend?" I asked Jim.

"Dropped hooks into water," he replied.

"Fishing, eh?"

"No, golfing."

"Anybody who can keep his eye on the ball is bound to be a success, especially if he likes golf."

—Unknown

Do You Play?

About four or five years ago I was standing in a ticket line at LAX, and a fellow in a line parallel to mine had a golf bag slung over his shoulder. Since the line was long and airline ticketing is a slow process at best, we struck up a conversation. He brightened when I admired his golf bag, and he proudly stated that he was on the PGA Tour. Then he turned to me and asked the question all golfers ask: "Do you play?"

I shook my head, "I used to, but I quit because I wasn't very good. I shot consistently in the lower seventies."

There was a long, low intake of breath, then, "The lower seventies?"

"Yes," I admitted.

"Consistently?" he queried admiringly.

"Every hole," I confessed.

"We have fifty-one golf courses in Palm Springs. [Gerald Ford] never decides which course he will play until after the 1st tee shot...At least he can't cheat on his score— all you have to do is look back down the fairway and count the wounded."

—Bob Hope

"I GUESS PRAYING ON SUNDAY MORNING
REALLY HELPS!"

👉 Holy One

A priest rushed from church one day to keep a golf date. He was halfway down the first fairway, waiting to hit his second shot, when he heard the familiar "*Fore!*" Seconds later, a ball slammed into his back.

Soon the golfer who had made the drive was on the scene to offer his apologies. When the priest assured him that he was all right, the man smiled. "Thank goodness, Father!" he exclaimed. "I've been playing this game for forty years, and now I can finally tell my friends that I've hit my first holy one!"

> **"Be funny on a golf course? Do I kid my best friend's mother about her heart condition?"**
>
> —Phil Silvers

The Borrowing Golfer

Every time the man next door headed toward Robinson's house, Robinson knew he was coming to borrow something. "He won't get away with it this time," muttered Robinson to his wife. "Watch this."

"Er, I was wondering if you'd be using your power saw this morning?" the neighbor began.

"Gee, I'm awfully sorry," said Robinson with a smug look, "but the fact of the matter is, I'll be using it all day."

"In that case," said the neighbor, "you won't be using your golf clubs; mind if I borrow them?"

"Relax? How can anybody relax and play golf? You have to grip the club, don't you?"

—Ben Hogan

"Indeed, the highest pleasure
of golf may be that on the fairways
and far from all the pressures of commerce
and rationality, we can feel immortal
for a few hours."

—Colman McCarthy

👉 Which Club

A golfer took his tee shot and watched the ball sail into the woods. His next shot went into a few trees. He tried again and managed to hit the ball over the fairway and into more trees.

Finally, after several more shots, he ended up in a sand trap. Throughout his ordeal, he was under the watchful eye of the local golf pro.

"Which club should I use on this shot?" he asked the pro.

"I don't know," the pro replied. "What game are you playing?"

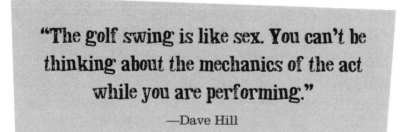

"The golf swing is like sex. You can't be thinking about the mechanics of the act while you are performing."

—Dave Hill

"HAVING MY UPS AND DOWNS, AND YOU?"

☞ Golf Again?

"You're going out to play golf again?" his wife complained.

"I'm only following doctor's orders," replied her husband.

"Do I look stupid to you?" she screamed.

"But it's true," he said, walking out the door. "He specifically told me I should get some iron every day."

"**Golf** is a sport in which the ball lies poorly but the player well."

—Unknown

Out Late

"What's your excuse for coming home at this time of the night?" the avid golfer's wife asked him.

"I was golfing with Tom and Ray, my dear," replied her husband.

"What?" she yelled. "At 2:00 in the morning!?"

"Well, yes," he explained. "We were using nightclubs."

"Playing golf is just like going to a strip club. You're all revved up, ready to go. But three hours later, you're depressed, plastered, and most of your balls are missing."

—James Clark

Echoes

A friend of mine hates to lose at golf. He was in a foursome when his ball landed in a sand trap. He was hidden from view, but the rest of us could hear him as he hacked away at the ball. When he finally drove it out and rejoined us, I asked him how many strokes that was.

"Three," he replied.

"Oh come on!" I said. "I heard six."

"It was a very deep trap," he replied. "Three were echoes."

"Never bet with anyone you meet on the 1st tee who has a deep suntan, a 1-iron in his bag, and squinty eyes."

—Dave Marr

I Sort-of Do

On a beautiful, sunny Sunday afternoon, Morris stood on the 1st tee at his country club. He had just pulled out his driver when a young woman in a wedding gown came running up to him, crying.

"You bastard!" she screamed in his face. "You lousy, no-good, rotten, damn, stinking bastard!"

"What's your problem, Sherry?" he calmly replied. "I distinctly told you only if it rained."

Wrong Message

The little church in the suburbs suddenly stopped buying from its regular office supply dealer. So, the dealer telephoned Deacon Brown to ask why.

"I'll tell you why," scolded Deacon Brown. "Our church ordered some pencils from you to be used in the pews for visitors to register."

"Well," interrupted the dealer, "didn't you receive them yet?"

"Oh, we received them all right," replied Deacon Brown. "However, you sent us some golf pencils...each stamped with the words, 'Play Golf Next Sunday.'"

☞ The Birds and the Bees

Comes the time in a boy's life when Dad sits him down for the "big talk." This was one father's approach:

"Son," he said, "you'll soon have urges and feelings that you've never had before. Your heart will start to pound, and the palms of your hands will sweat. You'll be preoccupied, and you won't be able to think of anything else.

"But don't worry," he continued, "it's perfectly normal—it's called golf."

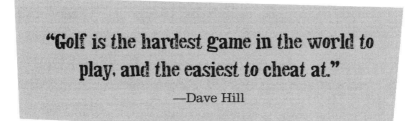

"Golf is the hardest game in the world to play, and the easiest to cheat at."

—Dave Hill

☞ What's Your Secret?

A reporter was interviewing Jack Nicklaus. He asked, "Jack, you are spectacular! Your name is synonymous with the game of golf. You really know your way around the course. What is your secret?"

To which Jack replied, "The holes are numbered."

"You know what they say about big hitters...the woods are full of them."

—Jimmy Demaret

To Golf or Not to Golf

Four middle-aged jocks were out for their usual game of golf. Seldom did any of these guys break a hundred, but they faithfully played three or four times a week.

One day Fred was having a particularly tough time, taking his fourth shot from the bunker on a 120-yard par-3. Frustrated, he expressed his feelings, and the feelings of his three buddies, when he said, "If I wasn't married, I'd give up this darn game!"

"The reason the golf pro tells you to keep your head down is so you can't see him laughing."

—Phyllis Diller

Famous Foursome

There was once a foursome playing that was taking forever to get around the course. The group consisted of Monica Lewinski, O.J. Simpson, Ted Kennedy, and Bill Clinton.

According to observers, the problems they were having were attributable to typical problems faced by the novice golfer... Monica is a hooker, O.J. is a slicer, Kennedy can't drive over water, and Clinton is never sure which hole he's supposed to be playing.

> **"My best score ever was 103, but I've only been playing fifteen years."**
> —Alex Karras

"Actually, the only time I ever took out
a 1-iron was to kill a tarantula.
And I took a seven to do that."

—Jim Murray

☞ Adverse Weather Conditions

Two blondes were playing golf at a foggy par-3 and could see the flag, but not the green. Each hit their ball anyway. When they walked to the green, they discovered one about three feet from the cup, while the other somehow had gone directly in. They tried to figure out which ball belonged to who, since they were both using Titleist number threes.

Unable to decide, they returned to the clubhouse and asked the golf pro for a ruling. After hearing their story and congratulating them both on their superb shots under such adverse conditions he asked, "OK, so who was playing the yellow ball?"

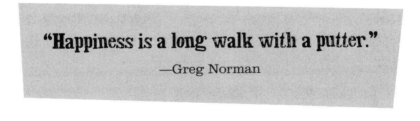

"Happiness is a long walk with a putter."
—Greg Norman

"I'll always remember the day I broke **90**. I had a few beers in the clubhouse and was so excited I forgot to play the back nine."

—Bruce Lansky

Putt

Standing on the tee of a relatively long par-3, a confident golfer said to his caddie, "Looks like a 4-wood and a putt to me."

The caddie suggested that he instead play it safe and hit a 4-iron, then a wedge.

The golfer was insulted and proceeded to scream and yell at the caddie, telling him that he was a better golfer than that and how dare the caddie underestimate his game!

Giving in, the caddie handed the gentleman the 4-wood he had asked for. He then proceeded to top the ball and watched as it rolled about fifteen yards off the front of the tee.

Immediately the caddie handed him his putter and said, "And now for one hell of a putt…"

"The fun you get from golf is in direct ratio to the effort you don't put into it."

—Bob Allen

"BEFORE THIS CRUCIAL SHOT,
LET'S HAVE WORD FROM OUR SPONSOR."

Daddy

One little girl was bragging about her father: "He must be one of the best golfers ever. He gets to hit the ball more than any of the other men."

👉 Smart Worms

Becky loved the game of golf but was not very good at it. She was out on the links one day, playing with her husband, Don. As usual, every time she swung at the ball, she made the earth beneath it fly every which way!

"My goodness, Don," she said, blushing at her ineptitude, "I bet the worms think there's an earthquake going on."

"Don't worry, honey. The worms on this course are mighty smart. My guess is that most of them are hiding beneath your golf ball for safety!"

"Nobody asked how you looked, just what you shot."

—Sam Snead

👉 Him and Her

A wife and husband both talked in their sleep. She loved auctions; his hobby was golf. The other night, the golfer yelled, "Fore!"

His wife yelled back, "Four-fifty!"

> **"When I'm on a golf course and it starts to rain and lightning, I hold up my 1-iron, 'cause I know even God can't hit a 1-iron."**
>
> —Lee Trevino

Golf Dog

A man and his friend meet at the clubhouse and decide to play a round of golf together. The man has a little dog with him and on the 1st green, and when the man holes out a 20-foot putt, the little dog starts to yip and stands up on its hind legs.

The friend is quite amazed at this clever trick and says, "That dog is really talented! What does he do if you miss a putt?"

"Somersaults," says the man.

"Somersaults?!" says the friend, "That's incredible. How many does he do?"

"Well," says the man. "That depends on how hard I kick him in the ass."

God and Moses

God and Moses were out golfing. They were both doing well. Then they came up to the 5th hole. It was a dogleg to the left, with a lake to the right. Moses got up and hit a long shot with a little hook right in the middle of the fairway. Then God got up and pulled out his driver.

Then Moses said, "God, every time you use your driver, you always slice it."

God said, "If Tiger Woods can do it, I can do it." He approached the ball, got ready, and then hit a long one. It drifted to the right, *splish*! Right into the middle of the lake.

Moses said, "See, God, I told you that would happen. I'll get it this time, but you'll have to get it next time." So Moses went out to the lake, held up his club, and parted the lake. Then he went down, picked up the ball, and came back. After that, everything was going fine.

Until the 18th hole, straightaway, with a long lake on the right. Moses hit a nice straight shot down the fairway. Then God took out his driver.

Moses said, "God, last time you used your driver you sliced it. You always slice it."

And God repeated, "If Tiger Woods can do it, I can do it." So he got up, and hit the ball. Long hard shot, sliced, *plunk*!

Moses said, "I got the last one." So God walked on the water, bent over, picked up the ball. About this time there was a foursome coming up behind them.

One of the guys saw what God was doing and asked Moses, "Who does that guy think he is, Jesus?"

Moses replied, "No. He thinks he's Tiger Woods."

"Golf is a game whose aim is to hit a very small ball into an even smaller hole, with weapons singularly ill-designed for the purpose."

—Winston Churchill

"I NEVER WANT TO HEAR AGAIN ABOUT HOW YOU OUTWITTED THE REAL ESTATE AGENT!"

He's a Liar

A group of golfers is searching for one of their golf balls out in the deep rough. After several minutes of laboring, the golfer who sliced his ball out into the trash declares he found it, inciting another in his group to scream out:

"He is a damn liar! I have his ball in my pocket!"

Rude Caddie

"That's it!" said the exasperated golfer to this insolent young caddie. "I've had enough of your lip. When we get back to the clubhouse, I'm going to report you directly to the caddie master."

"Ooooooh, I'm so worried," responded the little brat.

"You'd better worry," said the golfer.

"And why should I worry?" said the kid. "At the rate you play, by the time we get back, it'll be time for me to retire."

"Talking to a golf ball won't do you any good. Unless you do it while your opponent is teeing off."

—Bruce Lansky

Handicap

What is a handicapped golfer?
One who plays with his boss.

"I find it more satisfying to be a bad player at golf. The worse you play, the better you remember the occasional good shot."

—Nubar Sarkis Gulbenkian

"He enjoys that perfect peace, that peace beyond all understanding, which comes at its maximum only to the man who has given up golf."

—P.G. Wodehouse

Transfer

After Sunday service, a young couple talked to a pastor about joining the church. He hadn't met the husband before, and he asked what church the husband was transferring from.

A little sadly, he replied, "I am transferring from the Municipal Golf Course."

"Golf and sex are about the only things you can enjoy without being good at it."

—Jimmy Demaret

"Golf is **90** percent inspiration and **10** percent perspiration."

—Johnny Miller

Gimme a Break

A yuppie was sent a ransom note saying that he was to bring $50,000 to the 17th hole of the country club at ten o'clock the next day if he ever wanted to see his wife alive again.

He didn't arrive until almost 12:30. A masked man stepped out from behind some bushes and growled, "What the hell took ya so long? You're over two hours late."

"Hey! Give me a break," whined the yuppie. "I have a 27-handicap."

"CONGRATULATIONS, YOU GOT A BIRDIE!"

> **"The only shots you can be sure of are those you've had already."**
>
> —Byron Nelson

👉 Questionable Pro

"I don't know about that new pro," said Robby at the golf club. "He may be a little strange."

"Why do you think that?" asked Bill.

"He just tried to correct my stance again," said Robby.

"So?" said Bill. "He's just trying to help your game."

"Yeah, I know, but I was standing at the urinal at the time."

☞ Add a Stroke

Three members of a golf club were arguing loudly while the fourth member of their group lay dead in a bunker. A club official was called to calm the row. "What's the trouble here?" he asked.

"My partner has had a stroke, and these two bastards want to add it to my score."

"Golf is an ideal diversion, but a ruinous disease."

—Bertie Forbes

👉 You Must Be

A parish priest was invited to play golf with two friends. Although he said his game was terrible, he went along anyway.

At the 1st tee, another golfer joined them to make a foursome. So as not to make the stranger nervous, the priest insisted they introduce him as "Ron." On the 4th hole, the other golfer turned to Ron and asked him what he did for a living.

Confronted, Ron admitted that he was a Catholic priest.

"I knew it!" the stranger exclaimed. "The way you play golf and don't swear, you had to be a priest!"

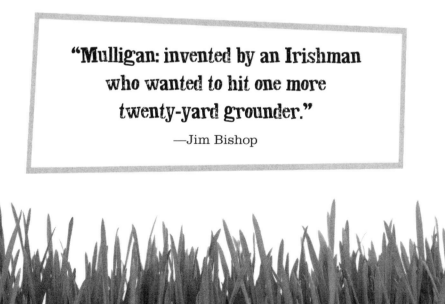

> **"Mulligan: invented by an Irishman who wanted to hit one more twenty-yard grounder."**
>
> —Jim Bishop

"...AND THIS ONE I DESIGNED FOR WEEKENDS."

> *"They say golf is like life, but don't believe them. Golf is more complicated than that."*
>
> —Gardner Dickinson

After Death

Michael was an extremely avid golfer with such a cynical attitude and arrogance, that when he passed away, few people shed a tear. Michael approached the Pearly Gates where St. Peter was waiting for him. Rather than pass through the gates as normal people had done, Michael stopped to ask a question.

"Before I agree to come in, I want to know exactly what kind of golf course you have here," he said to St. Peter.

"That shouldn't matter to you," said St. Peter.

"But it does!" And then, in his arrogant manner, he exclaimed, "Well, if I can't see it, then I'm not coming in!"

"Very well, Michael. As you wish…look through the gates." He looked and saw the poorest, most rundown excuse for a golf course. It made him sick to his stomach.

"Forget it! There is no way I'm going to spend eternity playing on *that* course!"

Just then, Michael heard the Devil calling him over the gate. "Come over here and see what I have to offer."

Michael peered through the gate and was elated! There was the most absolutely fabulous golf course he had ever seen!

He turned to the Devil and said, "Yeah…I want to play *that* course!"

"OK. Step on through, and it's yours forever."

St. Peter pleaded with Michael as he headed off with the Devil and the gates closed behind him. Michael walked up to the first tee and said, "I can't wait to play! Where are my clubs and ball?"

The Devil roared with laughter. "Oh that…there aren't any."

Golf Lesson

A retiree was given a set of golf clubs by his coworkers. Thinking he'd try the game, he asked the local pro for lessons, explaining that he knew nothing whatsoever about golf. The pro showed him the stance and swing, and then said, "Just hit the ball toward the flag on the first green."

The novice teed up and smacked the ball straight down the fairway and onto the green, where it stopped inches from the hole.

"Now what?" the fellow asked the speechless pro.

"Uh...you're supposed to hit the ball into the cup," the pro finally said, after he was able to speak again.

The retiree replied, "Oh great! *Now* you tell me!"

☞ Ford Cars vs. Golf Balls

What's the difference between a Ford and a golf ball?
You can drive a golf ball 200 yards.

"A lot of guys who have never choked have never been in the position to do so."

—Tom Watson

"The number one thing about trouble is...don't get into more."

—Dave Stockton

"The fundamental problem with golf is that every so often, no matter how lacking you may be in the essential virtues required of a steady player, the odds are that one day you will hit the ball straight, hard, and out of sight. This is the essential frustration of this excruciating sport. For when you've done it once, you make the fundamental error of asking yourself why you can't do this all the time. The answer to this question is simple: the first time was a fluke."

—Colin Bowles

☞ Bet for Strokes

An octogenarian who was an avid golfer moved to a new town and joined the local country club. He went to the club for the first time to play but was told that there wasn't anybody he could play with because they were already out on the course.

He repeated several times that he really wanted to play today. Finally, the assistant pro said he would play with him and asked him how many strokes he wanted for a bet.

The eighty-year-old said, "I really don't need any strokes as I have been playing quite well. The only problem I have is getting out of sand traps." He did play well. Coming to the par-4 18th, they were all even. The pro had a nice drive and was able to get on the green and 2-putt for par.

The old man had a nice drive, but his approach shot landed in a sand trap next to the green. Playing from the bunker he hit a high ball, which landed on the green and rolled into the cup. Birdie, match, and all the money!

The pro walked over to the sand trap where his opponent was standing. He said, "Nice shot. I thought you said you have a problem getting out of sand traps?"

Replied the octogenarian, "I do; would you please give me a hand?"

"I've always made a total effort,
even when the odds seemed entirely
against me. I never quit trying;
I never felt that I didn't have
a chance to win."

—Arnold Palmer

"It's the most fun I've had with
my clothes on."

—Lee Trevino

"HAROLD'S BEEN A CHANGED MAN EVER SINCE I HAD THE GREENSKEEPER MODIFY OUR PUTTING GREENS."

Witchcraft

In primitive society, when native tribes beat the ground with clubs and yelled, it was called witchcraft; in civilized society, it is called golf.

"My game is so bad I gotta hire three caddies—one to walk the left rough, one for the right, and one for the middle. And the one in the middle doesn't have much to do."

—Dave Hill

The Amazing Golf Ball

A golfer, playing a round by himself, is about to tee off, and a greasy little salesman runs up to him, and yells, "Wait! Before you tee off, I have something really amazing to show you!"

The golfer, annoyed, asks, "What is it?"

"It's a special golf ball," says the salesman. "You can never lose it!"

"Whattaya mean?" scoffs the golfer. "You can never lose it? What if you hit it into the water?"

"No problem," says the salesman. "It floats, detects where the shore is, and then spins toward it."

"Well, what if you hit it into the woods?"

"Easy," says the salesman. "It emits a beeping sound, and you can find it with your eyes closed."

"Okay," says the golfer, impressed. "But what if your round goes late and it gets dark?"

"No problem, sir, this golf ball glows in the dark! I'm telling you, you can never lose this golf ball!"

The golfer buys it at once. "Just one question," he says to the salesman. "Where did you get it?"

"I found it."

"If your caddie coaches you on the tee, 'Hit it down the left side with a little draw,' ignore him. All you do on the tee is try not to hit the caddie."

—Jim Murray

Invention

Many years ago, in Scotland, a new game was invented. It was ruled, "Gentlemen Only...Ladies Forbidden."

...and thus the word *GOLF* entered into the English language.

"Always throw your clubs ahead of you. That way you don't have to waste energy going back to pick them up."

—Tommy Bolt

👉 Riders?

After a round of golf, four ladies sat around the club house chatting.

Seeing the ladies, the pro approached them and asked, "How did your game go?"

The first lady, a brunette, said she had a good round…making the comment that she actually had twenty-five riders. The pro was a bit perplexed, not knowing what a "rider" was.

The second was a blonde lady who quickly chimed in and said that she had a very good round as well with sixteen riders.

The third lady then said that her round was average and that she only had ten riders.

The fourth lady admitted that she played the worst round of the day and that she only had two riders all day long.

The pro was completely confused, not knowing what the term "rider" meant. But because he didn't want to look dumb, he made a quick polite remark, wished the ladies well, and left.

He then approached the bartender and asked, "Hey, can you tell me what these ladies are talking about when they refer to 'riders'?"

The bartender simply smiled and said, "A 'rider' is when you hit a shot long enough to ride on the golf cart to your ball."

The Nasty Hit

Joe, a notoriously bad golfer, hits his ball off the 1st tee and watches as it slices to the right and disappears through an open window. Figuring that's the end of it, he gets another ball out of his bag and plays on.

On the 8th hole, a police officer walks up to Joe on the course and says, "Did you hit a golf ball through a window back there?"

Joe says, "Yes, I did."

"Well," says the police officer, "it knocked a lamp over, scaring the dog, which raced out of the house onto the highway. A driver rammed into a brick wall to avoid the dog, sending three people to the hospital. And it's all because you sliced the ball."

"Oh my goodness," says Joe, "is there anything I can do?"

"Yes, there is," the cop says. "Try keeping your head down and close up your stance a bit."

"**Golf** was once a rich man's sport, but now it has millions of poor players!"

—Unknown

Match Play

Bill and Bob, longtime golfing buddies, were involved in a match-play contest with the score "all-square" at the 18th tee.

Bill sliced his tee shot way left, and the ball finally stopped on the cart path. Meanwhile, Bob smashed his first shot straight down the middle.

"Oh well," said Bill, "I should get a free drop from there."

"Heck no," said Bob. "We play the ball as it lies." And so Bill did. After dropping his opponent on the middle of the fairway, Bill took the golf cart to his lie on the concrete path. Sparks flew from the cart path, as Bill made a few aggressive practice swings.

Finally, Bill hit the ball off the cart path, leaving a miraculous shot only three feet from the pin.

As the two met in the fairway, Bob commented, "That was a great shot...what club did you use?"

"Your 6-iron," said Bill.

👉 Water Hazard

Robinson Crusoe–style, the shipwrecked golfer made the best of his tiny island. When a cruise liner spotted his distress signals and sent a boat to investigate, the landing party was amazed to find a crude but recognizable nine-hole course that the castaway had played with driftwood woods, a whalebone and coral putter, and balls carved out of pumice stone.

"Quite a layout," said the officer in charge of the rescuers.

"You're too kind. It's very rough and ready," the goatskin-clad golfer responded. Then he smiled slyly. "I am, however, quite proud of the water hazard."

> **"Golf is a good walk spoiled."**
>
> —Mark Twain

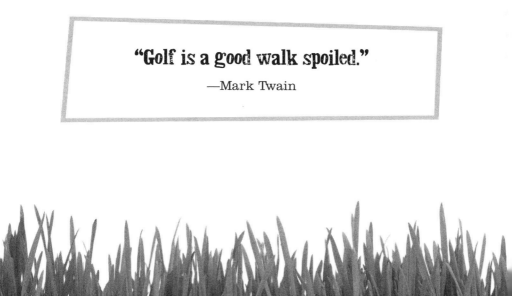

Doctor's Orders

"Say, Ralph, you want to hit the golf course this afternoon?"

"Sorry, I can't."

"Why not?"

"The doctor told me I can't play."

"Oh, he's seen your game, too?"

☞ Golfing Foursome

Four men were out golfing.

"These hills are getting steeper as the years go by," one complained.

"These fairways seem to be getting longer, too," said one of the others.

"The sand traps seem to be bigger than I remember them, too," said the third senior.

After hearing enough from his senior buddies, the oldest and the wisest of the four of them, at eighty-seven years old, piped up and said, "Just be thankful we're still on the right side of the grass!"

"I played like s—."

—Greg Norman after The Masters

Foul Language

Dave had tried to be particularly careful about his language as he played golf with his preacher. But on the 12th hole, when he twice failed to hit out of a sand trap, he lost his resolve and let fly with a string of expletives.

The preacher felt obliged to respond. "I have observed," said he in a calm voice, "that the best golfers do not use foul language."

"I guess not," said Dave. "What the hell do they have to cuss about?"

"That's what you play for, to separate yourself from the crowd."

—Jack Nicklaus

☞ Eight Iron

Off the 7th tee, Joe sliced his shot deep into a wooded ravine. He took his 8-iron and clambered down the embankment in search of his lost ball.

After many long minutes of hacking at the underbrush, he spotted something glistening in the leaves. As he drew nearer, he discovered that it was an 8-iron in the hands of a skeleton!

Joe immediately called out to his friend, "Jack, I've got trouble down here!"

"What's the matter?" Jack asked from the edge of the ravine.

"Bring my wedge," Joe shouted. "You can't get out of here with an 8-iron!"

"If you think it's hard to meet new people, try picking up the wrong golf ball."

—Jack Lemmon

> **"Competitive golf is played mainly on a five-and-a-half-inch course, the space between your ears."**
>
> —Bobby Jones

True Confessions of a Golfer

A man goes to the confessional. "Forgive me, Father, for I have sinned."

"What is your sin, my child?" the priest asks back.

"Well," the man starts, "I used some horrible language this week and I feel absolutely terrible."

"When did you do use this awful language?" said the priest.

"I was golfing and hit an incredible drive that looked like it was going to go over 250 yards, but it struck a phone line that was hanging over the fairway and fell straight down to the ground after going only about 100 yards."

"Is *that* when you swore?"

"No, Father," said the man. "After that, a squirrel ran out of the bushes and grabbed my ball in his mouth and began to run away."

"Is *that* when you swore?" asked the priest again.

"Well, no," said the man. "You see, as the squirrel was running, an eagle came down out of the sky, grabbed the squirrel in his talons, and began to fly away!"

"Is *that* when you swore?" asked the amazed priest.

"No, not yet," the man replied. "As the eagle carried the squirrel away in his claws, it flew towards the green. And as it passed over a bit of forest near the green, the squirrel dropped my ball."

"Did you swear *then*?" asked the now-impatient priest.

"No, because as the ball fell it struck a tree, bounced through some bushes, careened off a big rock, rolled through a sand trap onto the green, and stopped within six inches of the hole."

"You missed the %#$*& putt, didn't you?" sighed the priest.

👉 Golf and Taxes

Golf is a lot like taxes. You drive hard to get to the green and
end up in the hole.

> **"If you watch a game, it's fun.
> If you play it, it's recreation.
> If you work at it, it's golf."**
>
> —Bob Hope

> **"It is almost impossible to remember how
> tragic a place the world is when
> one is playing golf."**
>
> —Robert Lynd

☞ Heaven and Earth

Near the end of a particularly trying round of golf, during which the golfer had hit numerous fat shots, he said in frustration to his caddie, "I'd move heaven and Earth to break a hundred on this course."

"Try heaven," said the caddie. "You've already moved most of the Earth."

"I'm hitting the woods just great, but I'm having a terrible time getting out of them."

—Harry Tofcano

Is It a Sin?

"Caddie, do you think it is a sin to play golf on Sunday?"

"The way you play, sir, it's a crime any day of the week!"

Improvement

A golfer who was known for his bad temper walked into the Pro Shop one day and plunked down big bucks for a new set of woods.

The staff all watched to see what would happen after he used them for the first time, more than half expecting he'd come in and demand his money back. But the next time he came in, he was all smiles!

"They're the best clubs I've ever had," he said. "I've really had tremendous improvement! In fact, I've discovered I can throw them at least 40 yards farther than I could my last ones."

> **"Man blames fate for other accidents but feels personally responsible when he makes a hole in one."**
> —Unknown

"One of the best ways to help a man get out of the woods is to find the golf ball he's looking for."

—Unknown

"I play with friends, but we don't play friendly games."

—Ben Hogan

☞ Really Old Golfers

Two really old guys decide that they are going to try to play a round of golf together. They get to the 1st tee and the first old guy says to the second, "Can you watch my ball for me?"

The second guy says, "Sure! I see fine. Go ahead and hit."

So the first old man steps up to the tee and really hits it. He turns to his buddy and says, "Did you see it?"

"Sure!" says his buddy.

"Where did it go?" the first guy asks.

The second old man thinks for a minute, and says, "I can't remember."

> ## "Golf is like chasing a quinine pill around a cow pasture."
> —Winston Churchill

Female Golfing Terms

Caddie: Two women talking about a third who isn't there to defend herself.

Chipping: Time to get our nails done again.

Double Bogie: *Casablanca* followed by *African Queen*.

Fairway: Splitting the bill when the girls go to lunch.

Good Lie: Weight on our driver's licenses.

Greens: Lunch we eat when we'd really love a cheeseburger.

Hole-in-One: Time to get new pantyhose.

Iron: What guys need to learn to do to their own shirts.

Rough: Getting a guy to understand, well, pretty much anything.

Shaft: You watch the kids while he gets to go golfing.

Slice: "No thanks…just a sliver."

Tees: Putting on that Victoria's Secret negligee.

Water Hazard: Giving the kids too much to drink before a road trip.

Wedge: Bathing suit that's too tight.

👉 Naughty Wife

A man comes home from work and is greeted by his wife dressed in a teddy.

"Tie me up," she purrs, "and you can do anything you want."

So he tied her up and went out for a round of golf.

"As you walk down the fairway of life you must smell the roses, for you only get to play one round."

—Ben Hogan

Afraid

A business executive had retired and was discussing the joys of his new leisure time. During the conversation he remarked that he had been compelled to give up skiing, a sport he had enjoyed for many, many years.

"Afraid of injuries?" asked a friend.

"Well, now I am," he responded. "Before, I could drag a cast into work and still do my job, but now I'd be messing up my golf game!"

"Golf is an easy game...it's just hard to play."

—Unknown

"Golf tips are like aspirin. One may do you good, but if you swallow the whole bottle, you will be lucky to survive."

—Harvey Penick

"You don't know what pressure is until you've played for five dollars a hole with only two in your pocket."

—Lee Trevino

"One of the advantages bowling has over golf is that you seldom lose a bowling ball."

—Don Carter

☞ You've Played Before?

"Well, I have never played this badly before!"

"I didn't realize you had played before, sir."

"The right way to play golf is to go up and hit the bloody thing."

—George Duncan

A Heated Match

John and Bob were two of the bitterest golf rivals at the club. Neither man trusted the other's arithmetic. One day they were playing a heated match and watching each other like hawks. After holing out on the 4th green and marking his six on the scorecard, John asked Bob, "What'd you have?"

Bob went through the motions of mentally counting up. "Six!" he said and then hastily corrected himself. "No— a five."

Calmly John marked the scorecard, saying out loud, "Eight!"

"Eight?" Bob said, "I couldn't have had eight."

John said, "Nope, you claimed six, then changed it to five. But actually you had seven."

"Then why did you mark down eight?" asked Bob.

John told him, "One stroke penalty 'for improving your *lie*.'"

"If profanity had an influence on the flight of the ball, the game of golf would be played far better than it is."

—Horace G. Hutchinson

> "The mind messes up more shots
> than the body."
>
> —Tommy Bolt

> "The person I fear most in the last two
> rounds is myself."
>
> —Tom Watson

"**A really good golfer is one who goes to church on Sunday...first.**"

—Unknown

"**You can't lose an old golf ball.**"

—John Willis

A New Set of Golf Clubs

"I just got a new set of golf clubs for my wife!"

"Great trade!"

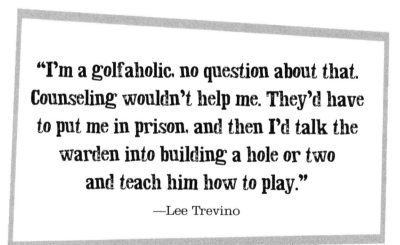

"I'm a golfaholic, no question about that.
Counseling wouldn't help me. They'd have
to put me in prison, and then I'd talk the
warden into building a hole or two
and teach him how to play."

—Lee Trevino

☞ Politically Correct

Did you hear about the politically correct country club? They no longer refer to their golfers as having handicaps. Instead, they're "stroke challenged."

"If you pick up a golfer and hold it close to your ear, like a conch shell, and listen—you will hear an alibi."

—Fred Beck

About the Author

Ray Foley, a former Marine, has been playing golf for way too long. Ray resides in New Jersey with his wife and partner of twenty-five years, Jackie, and their son, Ryan. He is also the father of three other wonderful and bright children: Raymond Pindar, William, and Amy.